4

Giant Steps
to
Leadership

4 critical skills

to transform your

people into performers

4 Giant Steps to Leadership

4 critical skills to transform your people into performers

By Ed Robinson

Published by
Rainmaker Press
A subsidiary of
Advanced Marketing Concepts, Inc.
San, Antonio, TX 78248
www.Edspeaks.com
1-800-381-14Ed (33)

Printed in the United States of America
ISBN 0-9745289-0-0 $14.85

About Ed...

Ed Robinson is an energetic and entertaining speaker, seminar leader and consultant. Ed's unique presentation style blends his career experiences, stories and up-to-date, targeted information. Ed's experience both as a CEO entrepreneur, and in corporate America, allows him to share real-life beneficial insights with his audiences.

Currently CEO of Advanced Marketing Concepts, a company specializing in business and professional development, Ed partners with clients to help them achieve better than expected results.

His unique presentation style and ability to provide a memorable experience keep Ed in demand across the country and internationally.

Dedication

*Thanks, to all my family and friends for
supporting me as an entrepreneur over the
last twenty plus years.*

*To my mother Louise
for creating me and starting my journey to
leadership. You're an incredible role model
for making a difference one step at a time!*

*To my three awesome boys,
Eddie, Steven and Big Al
for their unconditional love as well as
providing me with the juice to overcome any
obstacles. You guys are my heroes!*

*To Jo
for dancing into my world
and making my life
complete and congruent.*

*And to all of my clients
for seeing the magic in the message and
continuing to incorporate those principles
into their business and personal journeys.
You empower me and others
by the actions you take.*

Thank You all for being Giants in my Life!

Leadership ~

A leader faces reality - about people, situations, and products - and then acts decisively and quickly on that reality to get the results she/he wants.

This works for one reason: A leader sees change as both an opportunity and a necessity for growth. In the place of fear, a leader holds to his vision and moves ahead.

Conceive
and Believe

Napoleon Hill wrote, "What the mind of man can conceive and believe he can achieve." This wasn't merely a quote to Hill, but rather a personal philosophy of life. What does Napoleon Hill mean? He basically felt that the mind gives birth to our ideas, goals and dreams. As you picture your goals in your mind's eye, they are on their way to being realized in your life.

Leaders Give
Birth
to Their Visions
Everyday

They say that life is a journey and I agree. I would go a step further and say that leadership is not just a journey but also a reference, a collection of lessons learned through role models that we see and meet during that journey. Leadership is the accumulation of lessons that we observe and emulate, and it is these lessons that bring us to the point of growing into who we are today. Our continued growth will be forged by additional encounters, just as those around us (employees, co-workers, friends, children and loved ones) are forged into their uniqueness. Think of your own life journey.

As a matter-of-fact, I'd like you to do something. I'm going to ask you to close your eyes. As you close your eyes, I'd like you to think back on your journey. Think of some of the leaders that you've encountered in life that have made a significant impact on you and your life. Think of those leaders and then think of someone specifically. Who has made a positive impact to your life and who has contributed to you being the leader you are today?

Now write down those names.

_____

_____

_____

How have they made a positive impact to your life? How have they contributed to you becoming the leader you are today?

Identify three attributes these leaders had that helped mold you into who you are today.

Now write down those three attributes. Examples of a few are:

good listener, compassionate, ability to delegate, takes responsibility, honest, and fair etc.

_____

_____

_____

_____

_____

_____

As you look at these attributes, I want you to ask yourself if they describe YOU. Think about these as powerful words describing you. Those are some pretty positive attributes you've written down. These attributes represent people you've encountered: people who have made impressions in your life, in your heart and in your soul about what it takes to be a leader.

"

What the mind of man can conceive and believe, he can achieve.

"

~ Napoleon Hill

*A*ttributes of a Good Leader

I know that for you to be a truly successful leader, you must demonstrate many of the different characteristics of a leader. These four attributes (VCER) are paramount to a leader's success. Notice that these four attributes are interrelated.

- ◆Vision
- ◆Communication
- ◆Empowerment
- ◆Role Model

Let us dip deeper into the attributes:

The first attribute "V", means that a leader has to be a person of Vision. Lack of vision takes a person from being in front to the middle of the pack. Would you agree that vision is necessary? We will return to the idea of vision.

Secondly, is the "C", in addition to being a person of vision you have to be able to Communicate the value of your vision to others with such precision that those listening and following can take ownership as if the vision was their very own.

Third, is the "E", you must be able to Empower other people so that they choose to carry out the steps necessary to accomplish the vision.

Last, is the "R", you have to be a Role Model. You must WALK YOUR TALK. A leader has to model the behaviors needed to follow through on the mission at hand.

Based on these four key attributes I'd like to share with you some of the lessons I've learned that have helped me to incorporate those four key traits into my own life and my personal journey to become a leader.

Some say that leaders are born, maybe, though, I don't feel this to be true. I prefer to think that they evolve. People evolve into leaders as these key attributes are developed and acquired in our unique journeys.

$\mathcal{V}$ision

Leaders inspire and energize others to commit to their vision. Through their vision, leaders capture the minds of others. They instill a sense of ownership. They lead by example. A vision is:

- ◆ Customer focused
  - ◆ Clear
    - ◆ Simple
      - ◆ Unique

(Vision is forward thinking. Stretch your horizons and challenge your imagination!)

Let's go forward with a vision. Vision is the most powerful tool a leader can have. A leader must be able to paint a picture so that people are inspired to go out and learn new things – to literally become a greater person based on that inspirational picture. I remember reading years ago about a man with a great vision: Nelson Mandela.

Nelson Mandela became a leader in a world that had shouldered apartheid and he worked every waking moment to bring it to an end. Eventually, he would take over as a leader in a country whose politics he spent his life protesting.

One day at a press conference, a reporter asked Nelson Mandela a question, which drew the attention of all the other reporters.

I, too, thought that it was an inter-esting question and loved his answer. The reporter said, "You have spent the majority of your adult life incarcerated because of something that you believe in, but also something that you were not sure would ever come to fruition. But yet, you stood your ground and worked toward your vision and evolved into the leader you are today. As you evolved from prisoner to the President, what allowed you to hold on to your vision and endure all of those years not knowing any outcomes?"

I loved Mr. Mandela's response. He paused for a second and said, "I think I would have to blame my mother for that." They asked,
    "Why your mother?" He answered,
    "My mother taught me at a young age that there are three kinds of people in the world. There are people,

who do nothing, then there are people who talk about things to be done, then there are people who will step up and stand for what they believe. She said to me when I was a young child that, 'You will grow up to be someone who stands for what you believe in and you will make a difference some day.'" His mother evoked her vision to Nelson. What a wonderful encounter to guide him on his journey to leadership! Would you agree that Nelson Mandela's mother's vision of her son came to fruition?

Isn't it funny how the impact of our parents and guardians play such a powerful role in conditioning the person we evolve to be! I know myself, as we talk about role models and lessons we've learned I think back on the role models I've known and lessons I've learned. Another word for role model is *hero*, or in many cases, specifically mine, it would be *shero*.

"

You will grow up to be someone who stands for what you believe and you will make a difference.

"

~ Nelson Mandela's Mother

$\mathcal{B}$ig Ma, My Shero

Primarily my mother, Louise and my grandmother, Rosalie, raised me. Both were strong women! My grandmother was so unique! One might refer to her as the "Don" in the movie *The Godfather*. Remember how everything had to be blessed by the godfather? Well, in my family my grandmother was, the "godmother"; anything that you wanted to do, or even think about doing for any extended period of time had to be blessed by Big Ma. Big Ma stood five feet, one half inch and was deeply loved by family and friends alike. Big Ma and I had a special relationship, however it would be my guess that everyone she encountered felt special. We all called her Big Ma even with her short stature. Even though I stand six feet, five inches and weigh two hundred and forty pounds, she called me Lil' Ed. Hello! Yet all who encountered her, simply and respect-fully responded with, "Yes Ma'am." We all knew who was in charge!

The amazing thing about Big Ma, a power packed lady with a sixth-grade education, is that she was more sagacious than words can describe. She shared her snippets of life wis-doms with me. She said, "The more you do for other people, the more you help yourself." That's a pretty positive vision isn't it? Like the leader she was, she began sharing this type of philosophy with me in my earliest days. "The more you do for other people, the more you help yourself.", She'd say. The number one company you'd ever work for is yourself." and "If you maintain a continuous educa-tion mindset you will be successful and you can be anything that you want to be." Big Ma set forth the seeds of vision in my family and especially in me. I feel her philosophies and attitudes have sculpted a success vision for me.

I feel that by sharing your ideas with others you could leverage your progress, and that would be my vision for you. The extent that you believe and own that statement is the extent to which you can achieve it.

"

The more you do for other people, the more you help yourself.

"

~ Big Ma

Walter Helped Me Keep on Keeping On

One of my mentors is, Walter Hailey. Walter, an eccentric millionaire, believes that nothing is impossible. He believes that you can accomplish anything you put your mind to.

Walter lives in Hunt, Texas, which is kind of northwest of San Antonio where I live. For me to get there and visit with Walter, I must travel through numerous small Texas towns with names like Welfare and Comfort. Walter had an impoverished childhood. His first job was selling flour door-to-door and then he went on to selling insurance. Because of Walter's beliefs, that he could do more and be in charge of his destiny, he sold so much insurance that he bought the insurance company he worked for. He then turned around and resold the insurance company for seventy-eight million dollars. Walter always says that he sold his company back when seventy-eight million dollars was a lot of money.

Walter Hailey shared his vision with me in an extraordinary way. Like Big Ma, Walter created possibility and progress for me by sharing his vision. Are you creating progress through sharing your vision? As a leader it is your responsibility to light a spark of passion and vision in those you encounter and hope to follow you.

$\mathcal{B}$lind Bowling ... Communicating Your Vision

I've said that the first attribute is to have a vision and the second attribute is to COMMUNICATE your vision.

How important is it to communicate your vision? I suggest that, as a leader, you absolutely must communicate your vision in a way that generates energy in those tasked with strategically implementing your plan.

Here's a question: When was the last time you shared the top four objectives for your organization with the people responsible for implementing those objectives?

If you haven't shared the top four objectives for your organization with the people in it on a regular basis, you are practicing blind bowling. Blind bowling is a unique concept. If you're familiar with bowling, you know that bowling requires good vision. The concept of blind bowling, is when you go to a bowling alley someone puts a blindfold on you, gives you a bowling ball and tells you to knock over as many pins as possible. How would that impact your score? (If you're like me it may improve your score.)

Leaders often practice blind bowling in their organization. Often, I see people in organizations putting out fires: dealing with one crisis after another and not truly focusing on the key objectives. This isn't only blind bowling but it is also, majoring in the minors. It is incumbent on leaders to clearly state and reinforce their ensuing vision.

Do you have "communicating objectives" at the top of your list? Communication shares the direction, the scope, and the end results with the people. It shows them where to focus and how to get the best results. So, (to return to my bowling analogy) when they discover where the pins are, they can focus and deliver with full impact.

When we communicate objectives, people know what they're doing and where they are going on a day-to-day basis. They have a share in the vision.

*It is incumbent on
leaders to
clearly state
and
reinforce their
ensuing vision.*

Communication
Times Three

I'm going to share with you three ways that you can enhance your communication at all levels. First I want to ask you to focus on how you communicated today. For example, "Do you send out a memo recapping your accomplishments each quarter and naming your goals for next quarter." Yes, I know this is common sense, but we all know that common sense isn't common practice!

Let's talk about improving the way you communicate. I'm talking about you, how you communicate within your organization, with significant others in life, and with your children. What does it take to enhance that communication? My answer to that question is: communicate with a level of genuineness, love and empathy. If you communicate with a level of being genuine, a level of love and a level of empathy you will hit the bull's eye most of the time. Let's explore these three levels of communication.

Making the Connection!

What would you say it means to be genuine? Would you say it means to be a real person, or to be authentic? Would you agree that you can tell when someone is communicating with you superficially? When someone is not being genuine, you can see it clearly. They are transparent. The degree that we're not truly ourselves adversely affects our communication. The bottom line is that people will not believe an insincere you. If you can be authentic, if you can get down in the trenches and be genuine and sincere, *then* you can effect change in the minds of others. It's all about making a mental connection. If someone responds to the genuine you, you have made a connection.

*If someone responds
to the genuine you,
you have made a
connection.*

*F*ind the Love!

Secondly, in communication, finding the love is critical. Unfortunately, in the English language we only have one word that depicts love. The Greeks are more prolific with twelve words that depict love. Here are a few of them:

Philaous

There's a city in Pennsylvania named after this love; Philadelphia, the city of brotherly love. Brotherly love is a strong love. Brotherly love says that if your brother or sister falls off a bridge into deep water they can count on you to be there to save them.

Eros

Another type of love is eros. Eros is a kind of physical love you have for a significant other in your life. (That is a totally different book!)

Agape

My favorite type of love is agape love. Agape love is a non-judgmental, unconditional love. I paraphrase that by saying, "Wanting what's best for other people." If you want what's best for the people around you, in your workplace and your personal life, this concept will enhance your connection with them.

$\mathcal{W}$alk a Mile...

Let's tie being genuine and wanting what's best for the other person to a third communication enhancer, empathy, or being able to walk in someone else's shoes. I'll never forget the story about the old fellow who said that he did not know the difference between empathy and apathy and did not care. Wouldn't you agree that when we're leading people we have to realize that they have challenges in their lives too? Therefore we have to care too! What are those challenges? Don't be shy, be curious. Ask! "You have to walk a mile in their shoes", they say. I like to think of it as a dance. In the movie called *Hope Floats* with Harry

Connick Jr. and Sandra Bullock, Harry convinces a reluctant Sandra to dance with him when he says, "Dancing is just two people having a conversation!" You have to want what's best for the other person and demonstrate it in a genuine way. Complete communication is the only way you are going to be able to transfer your vision to others. When you show empathy, you can touch another's heart. By touching their heart, your vision touches the soul of the people on your team. That connection helps both of you get it!

When you show

empathy, you can

touch another's heart.

$\mathcal{N}$othing Less
than
One Hundred
Percent

The third key to leadership is the trait of – Empowerment. How can you empower other people to gather around your thought processes, your leadership skills, your goals, your bowling pins, if you will, those objectives that you are trying to accomplish? How can you instill the desire in other people to move forward? I feel it is fair to say that a leader must empower others to own and move proactively forward to realize a specific vision. This mindset is depicted in a quote that I love. It's by Ralph Waldo Trine. (No this is not Emerson's brother!) He states that, "Individuals carry their success and their failure with them. It doesn't depend on outside conditions."

Individuals carry their success and their failures with them; (their success or failure) doesn't depend on outside conditions. In my keynotes and seminars I ask participants, "Do you find that quote to be true in your life?" As you read this quote are you saying to yourself, "Ed, I buy into that." Perhaps you are saying, "Maybe yes, and maybe no." or "Well, maybe it depends on how you look at some of the individual meanings in the quote such as the word *success*." Would you agree that how you view success plays a major role on how you see this quote in your own life? I realize that a person's view of success and any value depends on their personal programming and conditioning.

If we explore that quote a little further the question comes up: How would you define success in your life, and in your world in general? Is it exceeding someone's expectations? You might say that success is the achievement of your goals or achieving positive outcomes, being happy, or possibly exceeding your own expectations. Not many people these days would say that money alone defines success. Would you agree that money isn't everything? At the same time, we all recognize that financial rewards and freedom mean something and are actually necessary to achieve many of the goals we want in our life's journey.

Remember my eccentric million-aire friend, Walter Hailey? Walter shares with all those he mentors that money alone will not make you happy, however, he says, "It can help you enjoy your misery in some real nice places." I love that! So, let's return to success.

Twenty years or so ago, working with the Chamber of Commerce at a networking function, I met a young lady and asked her the question of the day. "What do you do?" Her response was that she was a CFO (Chief Financial Officer) for a small but on going business. Awestruck, I said, "WOW! Tell me more. She told me that she was a housewife and mother of five. She had achieved and then communicated her definition of success.

What is your definition of success? Earl Nightingale gives us a quote that I call the essence quote,

"Success is the progressive realization of a worthy ideal." The progressive realization of a worthy ideal. What ideals make success worthy and important to you?

"

Individuals carry their success and their failure with them; it doesn't depend on outside conditions.

"

~ Ralph Waldo Trine

The Big A

The Big A is accountability; the flip side of the same coin is responsibility. To be successful, we have to start and finish with the Big A. Let's go back to the idea that we carry our success and our failure with us. I'm curious to what degree you find this idea to be true and applicable to you in your own life. "Individuals carry their success and their failure with them; it doesn't depend on outside conditions." On a scale of zero to one-hundred, I'd like you to write down a number. One hundred percent says,

"Yeah, Ed I'm with you. Zero says, "Don't quit your day job to sell this idea."

What is your percentage? Do you believe you create your own success and subsequently create a major part of your thought process for future success? On a scale of zero to one-hundred, how much do you find this quote to be true for you? Go ahead and write it down.

Are you there? Don't read on until you've given yourself a percentage. Now, I want you to write down why you feel that way. For instance, if eighty-five percent of the time you carry your success and failure with you, then what happens during the other fifteen percent of the time?

Many people feel that the deeper they delve within themselves, the more this concept approaches one hundred percent.

As for me, I feel that the level we incorporate personal accountability into our lives truly measures our ability to take responsibility when circumstances demand it.

Let's take this exercise a little further by going back to the quote and scratching out the word *individuals* and writing your own name. It would then read, for example, "Terri carries her success and her failure with her. It doesn't depend on outside conditions." Does that bring the idea of personal accountability home a little bit more?

Hitting Home:
Off by Half
a Million

Twenty years ago, I was a controller for a computer company. One of my responsibilities as a controller was to track the spare parts of our computers. We had about sixty-million dollars worth of parts around the world.

Gloria was one of my managers in the Logistics Accounting department. In Logistics Accounting, she would put together an algorithm every month, a calculation, if you will, that would tell us how much inventory we'd lose due to the shrinkage. After she'd do her calculation, she'd put it into a report and pass it on to me. I'd basically bless it and pass it on to my boss. My boss's name was Dennis. He was the Vice President of Finance and Accounting. Dennis would then take that report and publish it for the world to see.

Periodically, I'd scrutinize the report. This one particular month, I'm looking at the report and I realized that the numbers we had published the month before were off. They were off by about a half a million. Would you agree a phone call was necessary at this point in time? I had to call Dennis.

I said, "Dennis, the numbers we publicized last month were off by half a million dollars." I hear silence. You could hear a pin drop. Shortly after that I heard a click. He hung up on me. Shortly after that I hear a knock on my door. It was Dennis. He said,

"Ed, I don't think I heard you right. I thought you said that these numbers were off by half a million dollars." I said,

"That's exactly what I said." He became livid. He said,

"Who is responsible for these numbers being off by half a million dollars?"

I ask you now, who do you think was responsible? Me? Do you think Gloria was responsible? Was Dennis responsible?

"

*Success is the
progressive realization
of a worthy ideal.*

"

~ *Earl Nightingale*

Yolanda Knows

O.K., We'll come back to that story. Have you have ever been to San Antonio, Texas? It is a neat town. I've lived there now twenty plus years.

People from all over the world come to San Antonio to see the Alamo and stroll along the River Walk. On the River Walk there is a hotel called Plaza San Antonio.

There's a lady who works in housekeeping there. Her name is Yolanda. Now what do you think would be the responsibilities of a housekeeper of a hotel? More to the point, how do you think Yolanda defines success? Keeping the rooms clean?

One particular day, Yolanda is doing her job and she enters room 420. There's a business traveler staying in the room. This business traveler has placed various stacks of paper on the floor.

Yolanda comes to the conclusion that this gentleman needs additional desktop space. She calls downstairs and asks housekeeping to bring up an additional desk right away. They bring up a desk. She takes the papers off the floor and puts them on the desk. She makes sure that they stay in the exact same order. She cleans around it and goes on her way. Was that her job? Do you think that she went over and beyond the call of duty? Or are you thinking Yolanda should never have touched those papers?

As you can tell by now, I ask crazy questions, so I asked Yolanda, I said, "Yolanda, what would make you do a darn fool thing like that?" I was stunned by her answer. She said,
"PMS."
I gasped," Pardon?"
She said, "My Personal Mission Statement."

(What were you thinking? I don't want to know.)

I said, "Tell me more about this personal mission statement thing." She told me that her personal mission statement was to enhance the quality of the guest's experience.
She explained,
"Anyone who stays in one of my rooms, I want to make sure that they have such a wonderful time that they come back to our property and subsequently to my floor."

I looked at her and I said, "You know, there are some places you couldn't work." I continued, "There are some places that wouldn't respond well to your PMS. There are some places that if you called downstairs and said that you needed a desk in room 420, they'd say, 'You've got an hour to clean fifteen rooms. You don't have time to take inventory.'"

I loved her response. She replied, "You know what? I don't buy that because I'm in charge of me. I have choices. I can leave a note for this gentleman. In the worst case, I can go get the desk myself."

I think that Yolanda stepped up to the plate because she believed one-hundred percent in the truth of the essence quote, "Yolanda carries her success and her failure with her. It does not depend on outside conditions." Yolanda is not an exception.

This quote asks you: How much are you willing to take responsibility for your own success?

$\mathcal{N}$obody's Victim

Let's talk about personal responsibility for a second. If you're looking at a scale of zero to one-hundred, let's say that you're at fifty percent. That is that fifty percent of the time you take personal responsibility for your own success or failure. The definition of personal responsibility basically says that you are the principal source of the results that happen in your world: your career, your life and your odyssey.

Does that work for you? Now see, the flip side of that personal responsibility is also personal accountability: Is it not? You can't have responsibility without accountability. Accountability says not only are you the principle source, but that you're willing to take ownership of the results that happen in your world. You're willing to say, "I did that."

A leader has to step up to the plate because there are two sides to this equation. One is taking responsibility and having accountibility. The other side is not taking responsibility and becoming a victim. As victims, we become weakened as leaders and un-empowered.

Have you met that person; who doesn't take responsibility? They usually play the blame game. What about you? Are you a victim? Are you un-empowered?

…You are the principle source of the results that happen in your world…

I DID IT

When you work in an organization and that organization goes off and does something crazy, everybody in that organization is then painted with the same brushstroke. Arthur Anderson: Let's bring that up briefly. The whole Enron disaster changed how people look at accounting firms, internal audit, external audit and outsourcing in general.

Would you believe that all eighty-five thousand employees that were employed at Anderson were involved in the Enron affair? Absolutely not, but they were all painted with the same brushstroke, weren't they? In an organization when something goes terribly wrong, it is often the result of one or more people who choose to say,

"Boy, you won't believe what *they did to me* this time!"

To what degree do you step up to the plate and say, "I did that." I believe that responsibility is not pointing the finger of guilt. Responsibility is saying, "The buck stops here." To what degree are you willing to say, "The buck stops here."?

Let's go back to Dennis. When Dennis came into my office and said, "Ed, who's responsible for these numbers being off by half a million dollars?" What did I have to tell him? I had to say,
     "I am."

By the way, what percentage of responsibility did Gloria have? If I had one-hundred percent responsibility, what percentage did Gloria have? One-hundred percent? That would be two-hundred percent. Is that fair?

What percentage did Dennis have? One-hundred percent? Would that mean that when he came in and said,

   " Who's responsible?" I could have said,

      "Dennis, you are."?

   Would I be right? (Yeah! But you could paint a big letter *S* for "Stupid" on my forehead.) The fact of the matter is that I would be right. We have to recognize to what degree are we willing to step up to the plate and take responsibility regardless of who else is involved. Accountability leads us to the successes we have today.

   You may say, "Yeah, I'll buy into that." You may say, "It really does depend on how one defines success." I ask you, how do you define success in your life?

Have you been empowered through a vision such as Yolanda's PMS? As a leader do you communicate such a vision to empower others?

You might define success for your organization by saying that it means various things, such as: getting everyone involved, an outreach program, more programs to meet clients' needs, making more money, balancing what clients' employees and other stakeholders want and what you provide etc.

I think that we can help each other be successful. That synergy we create in a team can extend to each person. Individuals do carry their success and failures with them. As you share what your definitions of success are, recognize that other people have, once again, their own unique versions.

Success lends itself to many definitions. As Earl Nightingale says, "Success is the progressive realization of a worthy ideal." The progressive realization of a worthy ideal is an awesome objective in and of itself. Would you agree that it's up to you to determine what ideal is worthy, and what is your ideal that represents success? Not only for you personally, but also for the members of your organization.

I ask you, how do you define success in your

life?

Chill Pills

When I ask myself what represents success for me I can see that part of my success can be expressed in telling you that I am the proud father of three absolutely wonderful kids; three wonderful boys, Monster one, Monster two, and Monster three. I love them to death, and in some ways they are my heroes. My boys are 23, 21 and 16. They are the reason I traveled 150 thousand miles this year. My oldest son is married and has graced me with a daughter-in-law and two awesome grandsons. An old Chinese proverb that I love says, "True success is how your grandchildren turn out."

It goes further to state that, "Both grandchildren and grandparents have a common enemy."!

I often tell stories about my boys and lessons learned in both directions. Steven doesn't even have a name; people call him Son Number Two (Monster 2). It would be accurate to say that Steven is a unique individual; he's a very disciplined person. In junior high school, Steven had a dream of becoming a basketball player and tried hard to develop his discipline and… you know how parents are.

We parents have a tendency to caution our children's goals because they may reach too high. We want them to reach high, yet we try to cushion them from possible failures or setbacks. I was very much involved in "cushioning" Steven because he wanted to be a basketball star and yet

Steven is the shortest of my boys. He had great hopes of playing in college and subsequently in the NBA. In the eighth grade I started cautioning him.

In the eighth grade 180 people went out for the eighth grade basketball team with only twenty-four boys to make the final cut. The boys would then have two teams: team A would be for the "better' players and team B would be the second squad. I started murmuring to him, "You know sometimes it's political." I started to share with him; "Sometimes there are all kinds of things that keep people from being successful." As I'm cushioning his fall he said to me,

"Take a chill pill Pops." He told me that he had been practicing two years in anticipation of this moment. He made the team. He made the junior high team, then the high school team. He is now a senior in college and he's the co-captain of his team. To this day,

Steven still tells me to take a chill pill and I am arguably his greatest and definitely his loudest fan.

Recently, Steven illustrated empowerment again for me. My boys were going through finals this last semester, and I went to visit Steven expecting that he would be cramming and studying around the clock. Well, when I got there he was only casually reviewing! I said, "Steven why aren't you studying? Your grades are important to you, so why aren't you burning the midnight oil?" He smiled and said,

"Take a chill pill, Pops." "If I haven't studied throughout the semester, wouldn't you agree that cramming won't make a difference?" He explained to me that he had attended every class and took great notes, so he was not worried. Man!

I said, "OK. I'll take a chill pill." Later he said something that got me excited and all worked up again! He said this to me during a Spring Break. He tells me that his senior year is going to take eighteen months to complete. I think to myself, "This can't be good." I said, "If you're not cramming and you supposedly have everything under control, why is it going to take you eighteen months to finish???"

He says, "Take a chill pill, Pops. You probably remember that my school has two campuses, one in Dallas and one in Rome. Several of us have decided that we're never going to have this opportunity again. So we decided to extend our last semester and study in Rome. You see," he continued, "I wasn't allowed to go my first four years because as an athlete I couldn't leave the campus, so this seems like the most reasonable thing to do." (Parents beware of logical children)! I think, WOW!

We didn't even go into the financial aspects of this. You know what I did? I decided to take a chill pill. Then I started to realize that oftentimes in life we have to take a chill pill. Would you agree with that? Steven presented an idea that I am beginning to realize and that idea is taking a chill pill, or letting go a little bit. Letting go enough to be with the person, and allow the possibilities to grow. We often take this phenomenon lightly as we journey through life. Sometimes we lead best by getting out of the way!

...that ideal is...
letting go enough to be
with the person
and allow the

possibilities to grow.

So...

Now I Take a Chill Pill Every Morning

I have two numbers I'd like you to keep in mind. The first number is 3900. The second number is 1456. I'm not sure about you, but I am kind of a numbers and statistical kind of person. Years ago, I read that the average person lives to be about seventy-five years old. Some more and some less, but the average person lives to be about seventy-five years old. Its important to realize our mortality every now and then.

Do you have a special day or special time or place that you enjoy? I'm a Sunday morning person. I just love Sunday mornings. For years there was a song by the Commodores that had a stanza that went *Easy Like Sunday Morning*. On Sunday morning, I often wake up, play that song, then I enjoy the day by listening to some jazz, going to church and usually spending it with those I love or something I love doing.

It's kind of an easy day. I've realized that if we accept that seventy-five years is our average life span, then we have about 3900 Sundays to enjoy.

This past November I turned forty-seven, so as of that day, I have 1456 Sundays left, if I'm lucky enough to make it to seventy-five... By the way, I keep a giant jar of M&Ms to remind me of how short and fragile life can be. My M&M's are my chill pills...You need a chill pill every now and then. I like taking one every Sunday morning. You know, if you start with 3900 and every Sunday you take one out, it starts to diminish. How many Sundays do you have left?

The fact of the matter is that we do need to take a chill pill every now and then, but more importantly, in order to empower people we have to empower ourselves. We have to know what we value. Life is short. For me, I have less than 1456 more Sundays. What is your number? What about you? What's important to you? Where do you find your balance, where do you spend your time? What's important to you? Figure that out. Then, take the next step. Take a chill pill and then go beyond yourself. Recognize and tap into what's important to the people in your life and to your organization. What is it that makes *them* click? What is it that makes *them* get up on Sunday mornings?

To empower people,

we have to empower

ourselves.

We have to know what

we value.

Preachin' and Walkin'
Walkin' and Preachin'

The last key attribute to be a good leader is being a role model. Having and being role models are critical for all of us regardless of which stage of life we're in. Can you finish this statement, "Practice what you…"? Let me tell you something that's even more important than practicing what you preach: Preaching what you practice. A lot of people say practice what you preach to be a role model, but in reality, you can only preach what you practice when you have become *who you are*. It is who we are that makes us do the things that we do on a day-to-day basis. Who are you? Are you the role model necessary to assist others in growing? Do you model what you expect? Ask yourself, "Who are my role models?" To what degree do you emulate those who have empowered you?

One of my role models was my dad. My dad passed away when I was a young child. I remember one Sunday morning (I guess that's where the Sunday's come in) I had one of those days when I just couldn't find any-thing to do. Do you remember having one of those days? I remember just kind of mopin' out on the porch. My dad came out and said,

"Lil' Ed, what's the matter?" I said,

"I've got nothing to do." He chuckled and said,

"You know son, nothing happens in life until you make it happen!" There is a message there. One mes-sage is that nothing is going to happen in your workplace until you step out and make it happen. To what degree are you willing to make things happen? Are you willing to take the lead and make things happen at all? To make anything happen, you have to actually have an outline, a plan, an understanding, a vision of what you want to do. You must communicate a vision and then act on it: that's being a role model.

We often encounter leaders who are role models and they don't realize it. These are simply people whose every action reinforces their real vision. Decide now to make your actions congruent with your vision.

John is a role model. He is the Vice President of a major airline. I know John because every year I see him at instructional seminars for his industry. Every year he's sitting in the audience and he gets his people involved. Every year he contributes and volunteers his time and money. (It is said that where you spend your time and money is what you value most). He practices what he preaches as well as preaching what he practices. Would you agree that he walks his talk? It takes a rare person to not only lead a group but one who is willing to step out on the edge and say, this is who I am.

I had an opportunity to work with the IIA (Institute of Internal Auditors). A hero of mine leads this organization. While I work with many organizations throughout the year as coach, speaker, facilitator or seminar leader, it is rare that I encounter a leader like Bill Bishop. I say Bill is a leader not just because he is in charge, but also because he is innovative and passionate about what he does. He's committed to it. He's dedicated a major portion of his life to his profession of internal auditing. He loves his profession. Bill inspires others to become passionate about this profession. He truly walks his talk. Bill actually has "IIA" tattooed on his shoulder and over the years, he has talked to me about getting an "IIA" tattoo on my shoulder. While that hasn't happened yet, the impact of the man has made a mark on me. If Bill Bishop were here today, I would say to him, "Bill, even though I never put that IIA tattoo on my arm, know that the definition and the true character of a leader has been tattooed on my heart because of the role model you present on a day-to-day basis."

Are you a role model at your company? One of the things I'm suggesting is that you step out on the edge and do the things you want your people to do on a day-to-day basis. Trust me when I say this; if in fact you're not willing to do what you ask others to do, you're not going to get people to follow you.

Until you actually step out there and say, "What I am doing now is what I want other people to do."; it's not going to happen.

...step out on the edge

and do the things

you want your people

to do on a

day-to-day basis.

$\mathcal{A}$ Little Goes A Long Way

You can see that *who we are* and *how we live* day-to-day plays a major role. Let me share with you an interesting story about a young man and a young boy. Did you or anyone you know ever grow up at the YMCA? I am a YMCA brat. I can clearly say that my involvement in the YMCA changed my life. There was a gentleman at the YMCA named Dennis Ruble. At the time he was the Youth Director there. His vision was to take young men and mold them into leaders. Dennis did this by getting kids involved in the cadet and junior leadership programs at the YMCA. While passionate about what he did, he was very selective about whom he enlisted in his programs.

One day, a thirteen-year-old kid who came from a rough neighborhood was suspected of some wrongdoing. Little did they know that at the time this kid was under a lot of peer pressure. This kid was fighting on the way to school with a pretty rough crowd. This crowd gave him a choice of fighting daily or joining the gang. He finally submitted to being part of the gang. As part of the gang, he was tasked with various things, one of which was that he must go to this YMCA and rifle lockers looking for money or things to take back to this group of hoodlums that he thought were his friends. Every few days or so, this kid would open the lockers in the YMCA dressing room and take what he could. Eventually, he got caught by one of the junior leaders and they took him to Dennis Ruble. What Dennis said to this young man affected him for the rest of his life. Dennis Ruble looked at him and said,

"I've seen you around here quite a bit for the last couple of months. I've had various thoughts about you and there's one I'd like to share with you today." He said, "We have youth come through here everyday from all parts of town and every now and then I spot a leader." He continued, "You look like you should become part of my leadership program." He said, "You seem like you should be part of the cadets program because there are some real positive leadership traits in you."

Yes, that moment changed that kid's life! And yes, that kid was me. You see, good role models make a difference in lives to such an extent that this YMCA brat gets to stand in front of many people every day as a leader working to help other leaders grow.

Eleanor Roosevelt said, "Never believe that one person cannot make a difference in another person's life, because that is the only thing that ever has!"

You can effect growth in your organization, one giant step at a time!

Recapping the Love

If I were to summarize where we've been I'd say that the four key attributes that I want you to keep in your mind and heart are not only to be a visionary, but also to share that vision by communicating. As you share your vision you will empower other people to move forward. Last but not least, walk your talk, be a role model so that you can get other people to follow you to a better place, a better way. Be a leader, a visionary, communicate, empower and stand up as a role model!

*V*isionary

*C*ommunicator

*E*mpowerer

*R*ole Model

Your Attitude

Affects
You and Those
You Lead

I have had the opportunity to speak and work with many organizations, professional service firms, fortune 500 companies as well as government agencies throughout the US and in 17 different countries so far. I've found that the attitude we bring to the work place affects everyone, specifically those we lead and those who work around us. After speaking to well over 20,000 postal workers of the US Post Office, I've decided that they've gotten a lot of bad press over the years. I feel they are awesome people doing a tough job with little recognition. Without lingering too long on this,

I want to ask you this question: How much would you charge to take my mail to the other side of town, let alone the other side of the country? I don't know, but I would suspect it to be more than fifty cents or so. Yet, we ask over 820,000 people to do that with a minimum budget, and please know that our income tax does not support the Post Office.

Back to attitude: Years ago, I met one postal worker with whom I used to love to work and visit. His name was Ed Horn. Ed was always in a great mood. When I walked into the Post Office he would always have something nice to say. He usually called me "Sir" and then he switched that to "Young Man." I really liked that! One day I asked, "Ed, how is it that you are always in a good mood and always have a smile on your face?" Without missing a beat he said,

"It's very easy, Young Man, in the morning before I wake up, I reach out and I move my hands and arms around. If I don't feel a box I know I'm above ground and it's going to be an awesome day!"

It doesn't take a lot to have a great day does it? His attitude was contagious and all that encountered him walked away richer just because they came in contact with him!

No Worries, Be Happy!

One of my favorite places in the world is Jamaica! I guess I've been there half a dozen to a dozen times. I love Jamaica. As I talk about lessons and role models that create leaders, I recall my first visit there, when I met a wise bus driver. We were taking a bus from the Ocho Rios airport to our hotel. While driving, this gentleman shared with us the wisdom of the island. (I should say that first of all, before he started sharing wisdom he scared the be Jesus out of me. If you've ever been on one of those buses, it's a scary thing, so, by the time he began to speak, my adrenaline was flowing, and I was listening to everything he had to say!) "Ladies and Gentleman," he said, "Welcome to your holiday here on my island home of Jamaica! In Jamaica we have a different and easy attitude!"

He said, "Remember in Jamaica there are three things we keep in mind. First, in Jamaica we have a term called *irie* , which means *happy*. Everybody in Jamaica is irie and we want you to be irie as well, while here in Jamaica!

"Secondly, in Jamaica whatever you need we say, 'No Problem, Mon'. No problem.' Whatever you need, no problem.

"The third and last thing to remember while here in Jamaica is that most of you folks come from a very rushed life and you're here to relax. So whatever you want you typically want it yesterday. But in Jamaica we say 'Soon Come!'

Because whatever you need or want will soon come."

Jamaican wisdom affects me as a leader today. I recognized that life is too short to go through it in misery. It is imperative that we live to be happy! Too many people focus on problems. A leader searches for solutions and helps others find solutions to the challenges they encounter. Forget about your problems and focus on solutions. You'll hear a lot of noise about how it has always been, versus what it is and what it can be. Forget about the problems and focus on what it can be.

The last Jamaican wisdom is 'soon come.' As a leader, be patient. Recognize that the situation is not going to change overnight. Your organization will grow to be as good as how well you articulate your vision!

Finally, I go back to what Napoleon Hill said, "What the mind of man can conceive and believe he too can achieve." Good luck in achieving your dreams and leading others to the vision you have modeled.

Success to you on your journey to Leadership!

Be Happy!

No Problem!

Soon Come!

*W*hat Ed's Clients are saying...

"In addition to being inspirational, entertaining and relevant, Ed has an incredible ability to get to know us (his audience), making him the best motivational speaker I have encountered." ~ Judy Telge, CMC
Conference Chair TRACM

"I was totally inspired by your ability to communicate and motivate the varied personalities of our teams. Their excitement has enabled all levels of our staff to be more productive. You're truly inspirational."
~ Richard Terrell, Director
Advantage Rent-a-car

"Incredible how you transform a group of independent wills to a team rallied to make things happen. Thanks for being awesome..."
~ Brian Tramontano, V.P.
Merrill Lynch

"...our attendees thoroughly enjoyed your lighthearted approach in communicating the critical need for acceptance of responsibility at all levels...your stories have a way of not only being humorous, but also educational at the same time." ~ Yvonne D. Gaguire, VP
U.S. Postal Service

"

Incredible!
I highly recommend Ed as
your next keynote or
executive coach.
His keynote address hit sev-
eral key points that we had
outlined for our people. His
message left them energized
and ready to make things
happen!

"

~ Cindy Gabriel
Deloitte & Touche

*E*d's Keynotes

The Change Train: Get On Board!

Change: make it work for you! Shifts in your organization and industry are inevitable. Learn to revel in the opportunity of the unknown and embrace, not resist, possibility for your professional future.

4 Giant Steps to Leadership

Uncover your own meaning of success and powerful ways of being. The extraordinary gifts of role models illuminate valuable roads to integrity, clarity and ultimately strong, personal leadership.

The Rainmaker's Strategies for Success

Successful salespeople learn how to multiply their efforts and develop managers into rainmakers. Combine dynamite selling strategies with transformative training and create a succession plan that allows you to retire early.

$\mathcal{E}$d's Seminars

Team Building and Advanced Coaching

Leaders of today must accomplish more goals with greater results at a faster pace than ever before. In doing so, the leader is called upon to set and maintain a climate within the work group that encourages others to produce. Setting this climate and encouraging others involves High Performance Coaching skills.

The Rainmaker's Strategies for Success

Choose from 15 different modules of client development skills to design a structured process for developing long-term business relationships. A variety of interactive exercises and discussions prepares participants to walk away with a practical and usable process ready for implementation.

The Power of Influencing the Team

Influencing others through interaction and collaboration requires strong communication skills and strategies. This highly-interactive program assists participants in identifying communication and behavioral styles. Participants learn how to work with others to integrate ideas and create within their organization a respectful, collaborative and productive environment.

The Change Train: Get on Board!

Change is guaranteed; progress is not. Technology solves many technical concerns and often creates more. Our role as professionals must evolve to keep pace with the changes in the world. This program focuses on ways to cope, survive, and thrive through the myriad of changes we experience everyday. It brings practical suggestions to ensure that as the roles change, value is added to the organization.

Work, Life, Balance and Prioritization

Are you driven by your career? Do you often find yourself not making time for the personal relationships in your life? By developing and sharing strategies to alleviate the varied demands on your time, you will learn how to enjoyably get the right things done, at the right time, for the right reasons.

Ready, Aim, Fire.
How to Refocus your Projects

This presentation is designed to provide a "big picture" understanding of the essentials of project team success. The program models up to 12 skills and attributes critical to effective project management.

$\mathcal{E}$d's Order Form

Life's Lessons That Create Leaders CD

Send me _____ x $14.85 = _____

4 Giant Steps to Leadership Book

Send me _____ x $14.85 = _____

Work/Life Balance Workbook & Video CD

Send me _____ x $50.00 = _____

Team Building and Advanced Coaching Workbook

Send me _____ x $35.85 = _____

Conflict Resolution and Dealing with Difficult Behaviors Workbook

Send me _____ x $35.85 = _____

DISC Behavioral Profile with coaching option

Send me _____ x $75.00 = _____

Ed's fax: 210-342-4822
Mailing Address: Rainmaker Press
                  P.O. Box 780278
                  San Antonio, TX 78278

For more information on Ed Robinson
seminars, books and CDs

**Ed Robinson
Advanced Marketing
Concepts, Inc.
P.O. Box 780278
San Antonio, TX 78278
1-800-381-14Ed(33)
210-342-4866
E-mail: ed@speaks.com
www.Edspeaks.com**

Printed in the United States
91100LV00001B/22-219/A

9 780974 528908